Our Bodies

Our Blood

Charlotte Guillain

Heinemann
LIBRARY

www.heinemannlibrary.co.uk

Visit our website to find out more information about Heinemann Library books.

To order:

☎ Phone +44 (0) 1865 888066

🖨 Fax +44 (0) 1865 314091

💻 Visit www.heinemannlibrary.co.uk

Heinemann Library is an imprint of Capstone Global Library Limited, a company incorporated in England and Wales having its registered office at 7 Pilgrim Street, London, EC4V 6LB – Registered company number: 6695582

Heinemann is a registered trademark of Pearson Education Limited, under licence to Capstone Global Library Limited

Text © Capstone Global Library Limited 2010
First published in hardback in 2010
The moral rights of the proprietor have been asserted.

Edited by Siân Smith, Laura Knowles, Nancy Dickmann, and Rebecca Rissman
Designed by Joanna Hinton-Malivoire
Original Illustrations © Capstone Global Library Ltd. 2010
Illustrated by Tony Wilson
Picture research by Ruth Blair and Mica Brancic
Production by Duncan Gilbert and Victoria Fitzgerald
Originated by Capstone Global Library Ltd
Printed and bound in China by Leo Paper Group

ISBN 978 0 431 19507 0
14 13 12 11 10
10 9 8 7 6 5 4 3 2 1

British Library Cataloguing in Publication Data

Guillain, Charlotte.
    Our blood. -- (Acorn. Our bodies)
    1. Blood--Juvenile literature.
    I. Title II. Series
    612.1'1-dc22

Acknowledgements

We would like to thank the following for permission to reproduce photographs: Alamy pp.**9** (© INSADCO Photography), **11** (© shockpix.com), **13** (© Jochen Tack); Corbis pp.**4** (©Mark A. Johnson), **5** (©John-Francis Bourke/zefa), **22** (©Mark A. Johnson); iStockphoto pp.**8**, **16**, **17**, **23** (© Francisco Romero), **18** (© Terry J Alcorn), **20** (© Rob Friedman); Photolibrary p.**21**; Science Photo Library pp.**10** (Susumu Nishinaga), **19**, **23** (© Dr P. Marazzi).

Front cover photograph of a child with scraped knee reproduced with permission of iStockphoto (© Carmen Martínez Banús). Back cover photograph reproduced with permission of iStockphoto (© Terry J Alcorn).

Every effort has been made to contact copyright holders of material reproduced in this book. Any omissions will be rectified in subsequent printings if notice is given to the publishers.

Contents

Body parts

Our bodies have many parts.

head

arm

leg

hand

foot

Our bodies have parts on the outside.

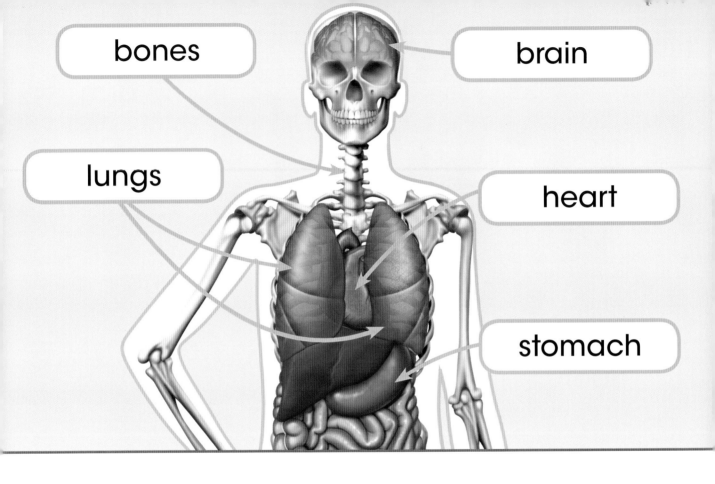

bones

brain

lungs

heart

stomach

Our bodies have parts on the inside.

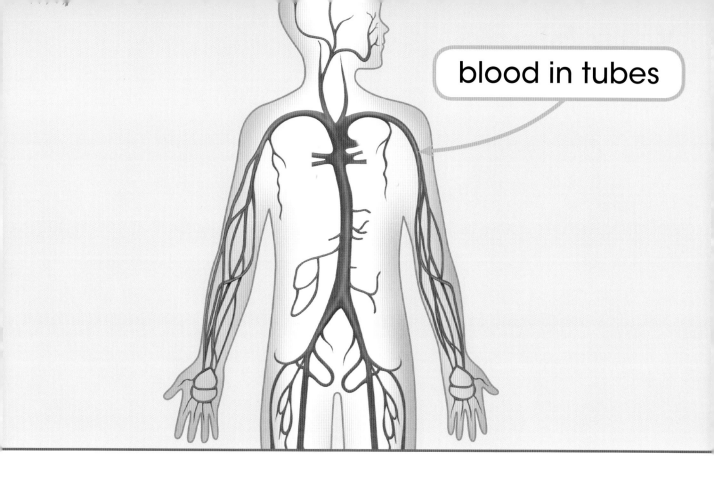

Your blood is inside your body.

Your blood

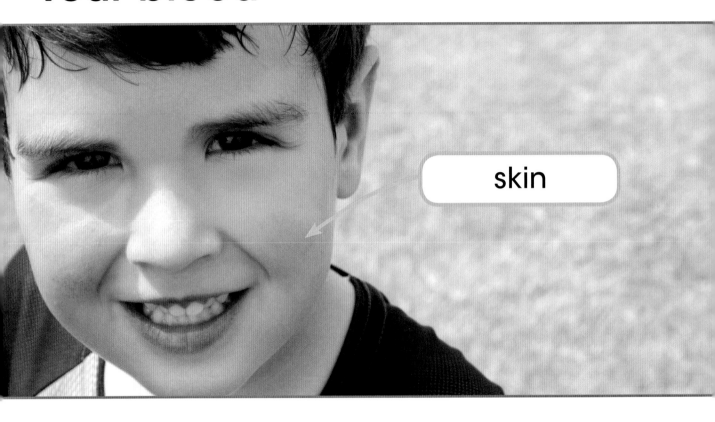

skin

Your blood is under your skin.

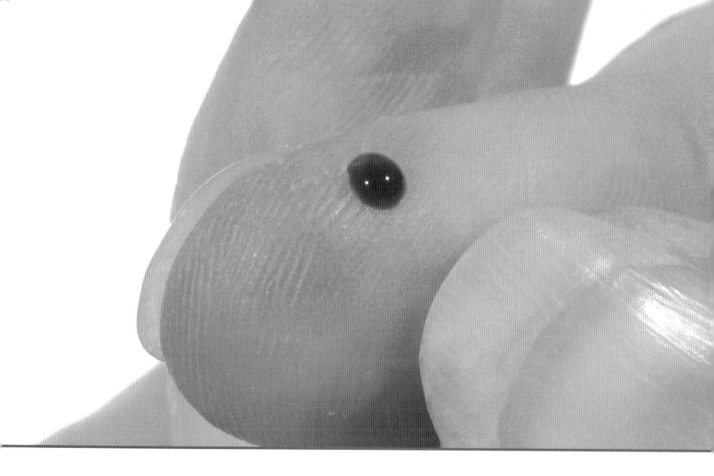

You can see some of your blood if
you get a cut.

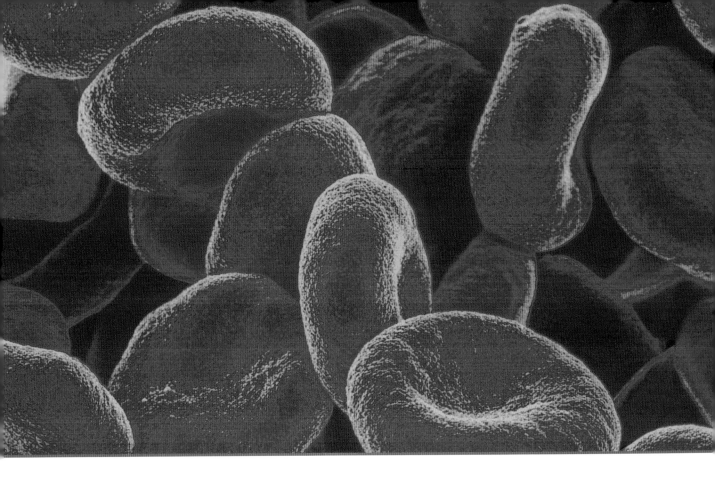

Blood is red.

Blood is wet.

Moving blood

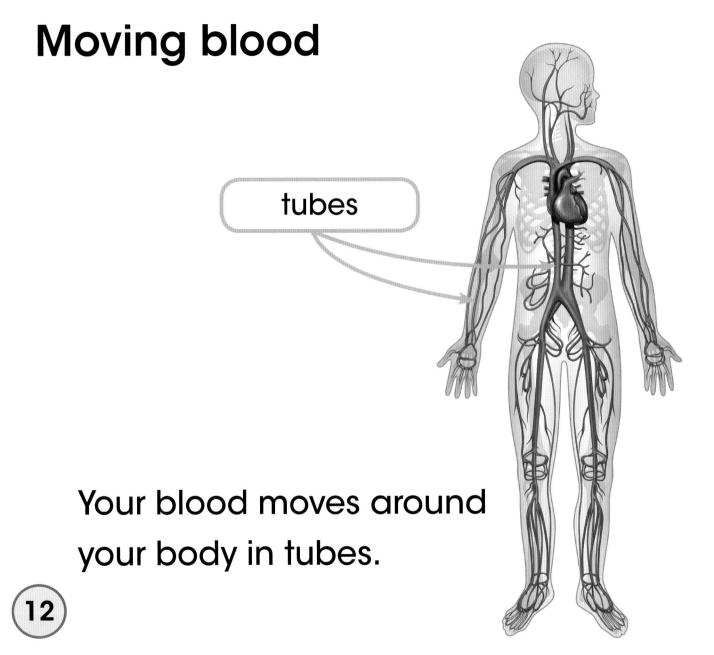

tubes

Your blood moves around
your body in tubes.

Sometimes you can feel your blood moving.

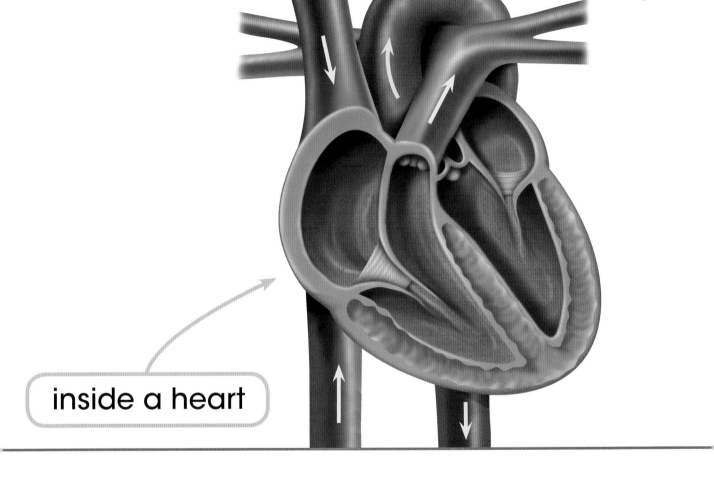

inside a heart

Your heart pushes blood around your body.

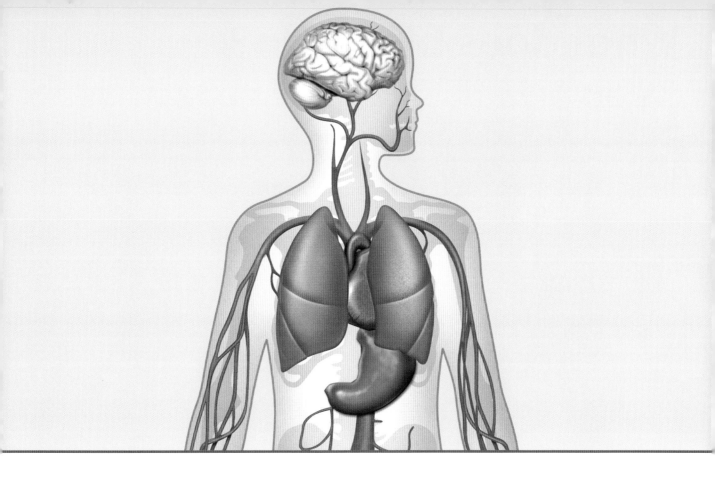

Your blood moves to all your
body parts.

What does blood do?

Your blood carries food to your body parts.

Your blood carries air to your
body parts.

Your blood helps to keep your body parts warm or cool.

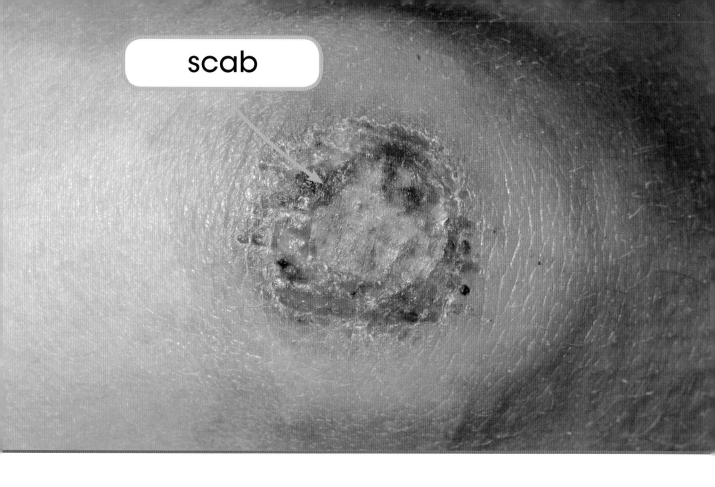

scab

Your blood can heal a cut on your skin.

Staying healthy

You can drink water to help your blood.

You can eat healthy food to help your blood.

Quiz

Where in your body is your blood?

Answer on page 24

Picture glossary

 **air** we need to breathe air in to stay alive. Air is all around us but we cannot see it.

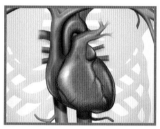 **heart** part of your body inside your chest. Your heart pushes blood around your body.

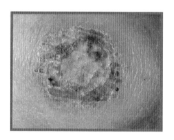 **scab** something your body makes to cover up a cut on your skin. New skin starts to grow under the scab.

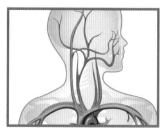 **tube** a long, thin pipe like a hose. Things can move along inside tubes because they have an empty space in the middle.

Index

Answer to quiz on page 22: Your blood is in all your body parts.

Notes to parents and teachers
Before reading
Ask the children to name the parts of their body they can see on the outside. Then ask them what parts of their body are inside. Make a list of them together and see if the children know what each body part does, for example, food goes into their stomachs. Discuss where their blood is and see if anyone knows what our blood is for.

After reading
• Take the children outside and tell them to run around for five minutes. When they stop, ask them to look at each other's faces: What do they notice? What else makes our faces turn red and hot? What is happening?

• Read *Ouch! I Need a Plaster!* by Nick Sharratt with the children. Ask if any of them have had an accident and cut or grazed themselves and encourage them to share their stories. Discuss what happens when a scab forms on your skin and what you should or shouldn't do to help it heal.